The
KIDS'
turn to
COOK

The KIDS' turn to COOK

Margaret Brooker

with Alexandra

& Charlotte Stephen

To Ken / Daddy,
the other food lover of our family,
with love and thanks.

This edition published in 2015 by New Holland Publishers Pty Ltd
London • Sydney • Auckland

Unit 009 The Chandlery 50 Westminster Bridge Road London SE1 7QY UK
1/66 Gibbes Street Chatswood NSW 2067 Australia
5/39 Woodside Ave Northcote, Auckland 0627 New Zealand

www.newhollandpublishers.com

Copyright © 2015 New Holland Publishers Pty Ltd
Copyright © 2015 in text: Margaret Brooker
Copyright © 2015 in images: Paul McCredie

A record of this book is held at the British Library and the National Library of Australia.

ISBN 9781742576893

6734

Managing Director: Fiona Schultz
Project Editors: Philippa Gerrard, Angela Sutherland
Cover Design: Lorena Susak
Typesetter: Peter Guo
Photographs: Paul McCredie
Illustrations: Rachel Kirkland at The Fount
Production Director: Olga Dementiev
Printer: Toppan Leefung Printing Ltd

10 9 8 7 6 5 4 3 2 1

Keep up with New Holland Publishers on Facebook
www.facebook.com/NewHollandPublishers

Acknowledgements

As my child consultants, advisors, peer reviewers and recipe testers, my daughters Alexandra and Charlotte have been key in the writing of this book. Much as they enjoyed the cooking, and the eating, there were times when they would rather have been playing than donning aprons to test yet another recipe. I thank them profoundly for their goodwill, sound sense and perseverance.

My appreciation, too, to Paul McCredie for his superb photographs. Unflagging, endlessly patient, and good-humoured, he was a pleasure to work with.

I am indebted to Kirkcaldie & Stains and The Homestore for the use of their glorious china that so enhances the presentation of the food in the photographs.

My thanks also to the team at New Holland for bringing this book to fruition.

Margaret Brooker

Contents

Why Cook?

There are lots of reasons for learning to cook. First, it's fun. You get to enjoy making the food and then you have the pleasure of eating it. And food seems to taste better when you've prepared it yourself. Plus, if you cook you can make the recipes you like.

Cooks are always popular. Your family will really appreciate your help with meals, and your friends will love to share in your delicious feasts. You can make cooking even more fun by asking your friends to help.

To be able to cook well is a major achievement. Think how proud you will feel when you serve a delicious recipe you have made yourself.

What's more, cooking is a skill for life. Knowing how to cook is an important part of learning how to look after yourself. So we hope you enjoy this book – and have fun.

About the Recipes

Alexandra, Charlotte and I have chosen the recipes in this book for two reasons: first, we really like to eat them, and second, they are easy enough for a beginner cook, especially a young one, to make. They range from breakfast dishes, to snacks, picnic and school lunch fare, main meals and accompaniments for meat eaters and vegetarians, and sweet treats (especially chocolate), and so cover most eating occasions. We have made sure there is enough variety to compose complete and balanced menus. We have even suggested some menus for particular occasions.

All the recipes have been tested by Alexandra, aged ten, and Charlotte, aged eight, and they all work! In our experience ten-year-olds are capable of making the recipes unaided, while eight-year-olds may need adult help. In any case, an adult should always be available to assist if necessary.

Each recipe is simple, and described as clearly and precisely as we could. We have given the measurements in metric and imperial as well as spoons. Make sure that you use one set of measures and not both because they are not interchangeable.

We have used ingredients available in a typical modern supermarket. However, we recommend buying meat from a butcher's shop so you can ask the butcher to cut the meat as the recipe says.

Sometimes you may not have all the ingredients listed in a recipe on hand or you may not like the taste of some ingredients so we have added the word 'optional' after those that can be left out without spoiling the recipe.

Each recipe makes enough to serve four people, unless it says otherwise; however, it is difficult to know quite how hungry people will be. The four people are assumed to be two adults and two children.

Secrets for success

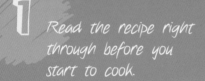
1 Read the recipe right through before you start to cook.

2 Check you have all the essential ingredients and equipment before you start.

3 Allow yourself plenty of time.

4 Wash your hands before you cook (see Food safety rules on page 12).

5 Measure the ingredients using scales and spoons.

6 Clean up the kitchen when you have finished.

Food Safety Rules

There are some basic rules to follow to keep your food safe to eat.

Be Clean:

- Wash your hands in warm soapy water for at least 20 seconds, then dry them on a clean, dry towel for another 20 seconds.
- Always wash your hands before you start to cook or eat.
- Always wash your hands after you have touched raw meat or chicken, been to the toilet, blown your nose, or touched a pet.
- Wear clean, protective clothes, such as an apron, when you prepare food.

Use Clean Equipment:

- Wash chopping boards and other utensils in hot soapy water and dry them thoroughly with a dry, clean tea-towel after using them.
- Do not use the same chopping boards, plates and utensils for raw foods and ready-to-eat foods without thoroughly cleaning them first. 'Raw' foods are foods that are going to be cooked with heat. 'Ready-to-eat' foods are foods that are not going to be cooked. They may be uncooked or already cooked.

Treat Food Safely:

- Keep raw foods separate from ready-to-eat foods. Store raw meats and chicken in the bottom of the refrigerator, so that no juices can drip onto ready-to-eat food.
- Rinse fruit and vegetables in clean water before use.
- Always cover stored food – whether it is in the refrigerator or in a cupboard.
- Always place leftovers in the refrigerator; if they are hot wait until they are cool.
- Keep 'high risk' foods in the refrigerator, for example, meat, chicken, eggs, fish, milk, cooked rice, prepared salads.
- Always thaw/defrost food in the refrigerator.
- Never re-freeze thawed food.
- Re-heat leftovers until steaming hot right through, and do not reheat more than once.

How To:

Slice a Chilli

- Cut off the stem, then cut the chilli in half lengthways. If you don't want the recipe to be too hot, scrape out the seeds and the white membrane that attaches the seeds inside the chilli and discard.

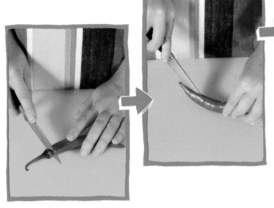

- Slice the chilli thinly crossways. Be very careful not to rub your eyes because any chilli on your hands will make them sting. Wash your hands thoroughly.

Peel Garlic

- Pull a clove of garlic away from the bulb (a bulb is lots of cloves joined together).
- Slice off a sliver from both ends of the clove.
- Pull off the dry, papery skin and discard. If it is still hard to remove, make a shallow cut along the garlic to make it easier to pull off the skin.

Taste Test

- Hold a teaspoon in one hand and with the stirring spoon in the other hand scoop out a little of the mixture.
- Transfer the mixture from the stirring spoon to the teaspoon.
- Taste the mixture on the teaspoon. Decide if the mixture needs more flavouring such as salt, pepper, or sugar.

This method avoids putting a spoon back in the mixture that has already been in your mouth.

Grate (Shred) Food

- Hold whatever food you are grating in your writing hand and hold the grater in your other hand.
- Making sure that your fingers are nowhere near the actual grater, slide the food down the side of the grater.
- Repeat again and again.

When there is only a small piece of food left to grate – stop, otherwise you risk grating your fingers.

Chop an Onion

- Cut the onion in half lengthways through the root (the hairy part).
- Trim (cut) off the hairy part and the stem part, if any, at the other end.
- Peel off the outer layer or layers of dry brown skin and discard.
- Place the cut, flat side of an onion half on a chopping board. Starting at the side, slice from the root to the other end, without cutting through the root. Continue slicing lengthways until the other side of the onion half is reached.
- Starting at the end farthest away from the root, slice the onion half crossways.
- Repeat slicing crossways until the root end is reached.
- Repeat slicing lengthways, then crossways with the other half of the onion.

Now the onion is chopped.

How To:

Squeeze a Lemon
- Cut the lemon in half crossways through the middle.
- Position the centre of the cut surface of the lemon half over a lemon-squeezer and twist it back and forth, pressing down on it at the same time. The juice will be squeezed out.

Make Honey Runny (Liquid)
Measure the solid honey into a small bowl and melt on low power in the microwave for 10 seconds, or place the honey in a small saucepan and melt over a low heat for a short while.

Separate an Egg
You will need a saucer, a small glass, a knife and a small bowl.

- Holding the egg over the saucer, tap the egg in the middle crossways with the blunt edge of the knife blade.
- Pull the two halves of the eggshell apart and tip the whole egg onto the saucer. The yolk must stay unbroken.
- Place the mouth of the glass over the egg yolk, being careful not to pinch it.
- Holding the glass firmly over the egg yolk, lift the saucer and tilt it over the bowl so that the egg white slides into the bowl.
- Place the saucer down, lift the glass off the yolk, then place it over the yolk again and tip the remaining egg white into the bowl.

Note: If you break the egg yolk, save the yolk and the white for another recipe and start again with another egg and a clean saucer and glass.

Fold Mixture

Use a metal spoon.

- Cut into the mixture in the centre of the bowl with the edge of the spoon.
- When the spoon reaches the bottom of the bowl, twist your wrist to scoop the mixture and bring the spoon up towards you. As you do this, turn the mixture over from bottom to top.
- Continue to cut, scoop and turn, turning the bowl around a little each time.

Note:
A number of recipes in the book call for plain flour. Plain flour is all-purpose white flour. Do not confuse it with self-raising flour, which contains baking powder ingredients.

Chop Parsley or Other Herbs

Wash the herb, squeeze it dry in some paper towel, then pick the leaves off the stalks. Chop the leaves with a sharp knife.

Beat Egg Whites stiff

Always use a very clean, completely dry glass or china bowl.
There must be no egg yolk in the egg whites.

- Using a clean dry whisk or eggbeater, beat the egg whites in the dry bowl. The bubbles will become smaller, the volume bigger, and the colour whiter as more air is beaten in.
- Dip the end of the whisk or beater in the beaten egg white and hold it up so that the dipped end is facing upwards.
- When the dipped egg white curls over, it has reached 'soft peak' stage.
- If you beat it more, and the dipped egg white points straight up, it has reached 'stiff peak' stage.

How To:

Melt Chocolate

Cut or break chocolate into even-sized pieces and place in a small bowl.

There are two methods.

Method 1: Put some water in a saucepan and bring to the boil. Set the bowl of chocolate pieces over the saucepan until melted; it should rest on the rim of the saucepan and its base should not touch the boiling water.

Method 2: Place the bowl of chocolate pieces in the microwave and heat on medium power for 20–30 seconds at a time until melted.

Soften Butter

Measure the butter into a small bowl, cover with a small plate or some cling film (plastic wrap) and soften on low power in the microwave for 20–40 seconds, or sit the bowl briefly in a sink of hot water.

Cook Rice

1 Put the rice in the sieve and wash well under cold running water over the sink. Tip the washed rice into the saucepan.
2 Add water to the rice.
3 Bring the rice gradually to the boil over a medium heat, then let it simmer until the level of the water is the same as the level of the rice and the bubbles are on top of the rice. Some people call this stage 'craters of the moon'.
4 Place the lid on the saucepan and turn off the heat. Leave the saucepan with the lid on for at least 20 minutes – do not take it off even to peek. The rice will continue to cook.
5 After 20 minutes, lift off the lid and stir the rice gently with a fork to fluff it up. Replace the lid to keep the rice warm until it is served.

Note:
Leftover rice can be stored in a sealed plastic container and frozen for later use.

Menu Ideas

Team up the recipes to create a whole meal. Below are some suggestions for various occasions. To make a balanced menu, we have sometimes suggested, in italics, extra vegetables or fresh fruit for serving alongside.

Mother's Day Breakfast
Bircher Muesli
Scrambled Eggs

Sleepover Breakfast
Pancakes or French Toast

Out-of-the-Ordinary Breakfast
Rice Pudding
Boiled Eggs

Packed Lunch
Sushi
Fruity Oat Slice
Fresh Fruit

Warming Winter Lunch
Tuscan Vegetable Soup
Cupcakes

Cool Lunch for Hot Days
Cold Soba Noodles
Strawberry Ice Cream

Afternoon Tea
Crostini
Cupcakes or Peanut Butter Biscuits

Feast for Friends
Guacamole
Spare Ribs or Chicken Nibbles
Roast Potatoes
Broccoli Cheese
Chocolate Mousse

Father's Day Dinner
Roast Chicken
Roast Potatoes
Cauliflower Cheese or Broccoli Cheese
Plain Carrots
Apple Crumble

Vegetarian Dinner
Dhal with Rice
Green Vegetables
Chocolate Sauce (with Ice Cream and/or *Fresh Fruit*)

Family Dinner
Baked Beans with Sausages
Green Vegetables
Filo Apple Pie

Birthday Treat
Pasta with Tomato Sauce
Spare Ribs
Vegetables or Salad
Chocolate Cake with Chocolate Sauce

Bircher Muesli

Serves 4

A delicious and healthy breakfast. It is just as good with fruits and nuts, or on its own.

Ingredients:

100 g (3½ oz) rolled oats

250 ml (8 fl oz) milk

125 ml (4 fl oz) plain, unsweetened yogurt

2 teaspoons liquid honey*

2 apples

extra fresh fruit, such as strawberries, banana, kiwi fruit, blueberries, chopped if large (optional)

3 tablespoons chopped nuts, such as almonds, hazelnuts or macadamia nuts (optional)

Equipment:

kitchen scales and measures

1 medium bowl

1 teaspoon

1 vegetable peeler

1 vegetable knife

1 grater

1 Measure the rolled oats into the bowl.

2 Add the milk and the yoghurt to the rolled oats, then mix them together.

3 Drizzle the honey over the mixture and stir in.

4 Peel the apples, cut into quarters, cut out the cores, then coarsely grate.*

5 Add the grated apple to the rolled oats mixture. This is the basic muesli recipe.

6 If you like, stir in the fresh fruit and nuts.

7 Serve.

*See How To on pages 15-16.

Porridge

Serves 4

Ingredients:

1 litre (1¾ pints) cold water

100 g (3 ½ oz) medium oatmeal or
rolled oats

½ teaspoon salt

milk, brown sugar, honey, chopped fruit
for serving (optional)

Equipment:

1 medium saucepan

kitchen scales and measures

1 wooden spoon

1 teaspoon

Charlotte loves hot porridge with fresh fruit on top for breakfast, especially on cold mornings. It's delicious, too, drizzled with honey or sprinkled with brown sugar.

1. Put the water in the saucepan and bring to the boil.
2. Sprinkle the oatmeal or oats onto the boiling water, stirring with the wooden spoon as you do so.
3. Continue to stir the mixture until it starts to bubble again, then simmer for about 20 minutes, stirring occasionally. As the porridge simmers it will become thicker.
4. After it has been simmering for about 10 minutes, stir in the salt.
5. Serve hot in bowls with milk, or if you like, sprinkle a little brown sugar, drizzle some honey, or scatter fruit over the top.

Scrambled Eggs

Serves 4

Ingredients:

8 eggs

4 tablespoons milk (whole (full fat) milk is best)

salt

black pepper

chopped fresh parsley or chives (optional)

30 g (1 oz) butter

toasted bread, for serving (optional)

Equipment:

1 medium bowl

1 tablespoon

1 whisk or fork

1 sharp knife or kitchen scissors (optional)

1 medium saucepan

1 wooden spoon

These are great for breakfast, lunch or dinner. Scrambled eggs are often served on hot toast. For a special treat, top the cooked eggs with pieces of smoked salmon – Alexandra's favourite way.

1 Break the eggs into the bowl. Add the milk, salt and pepper, then whisk together with a whisk or fork.

2 If using parsley or chives, chop or snip them with scissors and set aside. (If you are going to serve the eggs on toast, make the toast now.)

3 Melt the butter in the saucepan over a medium heat. Add the egg mixture and stir with the wooden spoon constantly and gently so that the egg moves around the saucepan. When the egg has thickened but is still creamy take it off the heat – remember that it will continue to cook with the heat from the saucepan.

4 Stir in the chopped parsley or chives, if using.

5 Pile the scrambled eggs onto plates and serve immediately.

Boiled Eggs

Ingredients:

egg/s

Equipment:

1 small or medium saucepan –
   depending on how many eggs you
   are cooking

timer or clock

1 large metal spoon

The method is the same for boiling one or several eggs, and for soft- and hard-boiled eggs. Soft-boiled eggs make an easy light meal, whether for breakfast, lunch or dinner, and hard-boiled eggs go well in salads and packed lunches.

1 Place the egg/s into the saucepan and cover with cold water.
2 Bring the water and egg/s to the boil over a medium heat, then simmer for the required time:
   o For eggs with runny yolks, simmer for $3^1/_2$ minutes once the water boils.
   o For eggs with soft but not runny yolks, simmer for 4 minutes once the water boils.
   o For hard-boiled eggs with moist yolks, simmer for 5 minutes once the water boils.
3 As soon as the time is up, lift the egg/s out of the water with the metal spoon, taking care not to burn yourself.

To serve:

Soft-boiled eggs: place each egg in an eggcup, cut off the top with a knife and scoop out the egg with a teaspoon. Soft-boiled eggs are good with a little salt and some fingers of toast.

Hard-boiled eggs: have a bowl of cold water ready so that when you lift the eggs from the boiling water, you can lower them immediately into the cold water. Leave eggs to cool, then, when ready to use, crack the shells and peel them.

Pancakes

Serves 4

Ingredients:

225 g (8 oz) plain (all-purpose) flour

4 teaspoons baking powder

½ teaspoon salt

1 tablespoon sugar

2 eggs

500 ml (17 fl oz) milk

2 tablespoons vegetable oil

butter, for greasing frying pan

maple syrup, lemon, sugar or lemon curd
   for serving

Equipment:

2 medium bowls

1 sieve

kitchen scales and measures

1 wooden spoon

1 frying pan

ladle

1 fish slice

Although pancakes are really popular for breakfast, they can also be eaten for dessert. They are delicious with maple syrup, raspberry sauce, a dollop of lemon curd, or sprinkled with sugar and a squeeze of lemon juice.

1   Sift the flour, baking powder and salt together into one of the bowls, then stir in the sugar.

2   Break the eggs into the other bowl. Add the milk and vegetable oil, then beat them together with the wooden spoon.

3   Add the egg mixture to the flour mixture and stir with the wooden spoon until the mixture is just combined, but still slightly lumpy.

4   Melt about a teaspoon of butter in the frying pan and spread it around the base of the pan with the fish slice.

5   Pour a ladle of the pancake mixture into the frying pan and cook over a medium heat. When bubbles appear on the top of the pancake and the edges start to go firm, slide the fish slice underneath and turn the pancake over to cook on the other side until golden brown. You can lift up the edge of the pancake with the fish slice and peek to see when the second side is ready. When the pancake is golden brown, lift it out of the pan and transfer to a plate. Keep the pancakes in a warm oven while you make the rest. Stack them one on top of the other.

6   Repeat the process with the rest of the mixture, greasing the pan with more butter in between pancakes.

7   Serve warm with the topping of your choice.

French Toast

Serves 4-6

Ingredients:

2 eggs

125 ml (4 fl oz) milk (whole (full fat) milk is best)

2 pinches of ground cinnamon

6 slices thick white bread (slightly stale bread is best)

butter, for greasing frying pan

caster (superfine) sugar, ground cinnamon or maple syrup for serving

Equipment:

1 medium bowl

1 fork or whisk

kitchen scales and measures

1 bread board

1 bread knife

1 teaspoon

1 frying pan

1 fish slice

Note:

If you want to make French toast for 2 people, then halve the ingredients (1 egg, 60 ml (2 fl oz) milk, 3 slices bread, 1 pinch of ground cinnamon).

French toast uses standard breakfast foods – bread, butter, eggs and milk – to make an extra delicious breakfast.

1 Break the eggs into the bowl and whisk with a fork or whisk.

2 Add the milk and cinnamon, then whisk together.

3 Cut the bread slices in half.

4 Melt about a teaspoon of butter in the frying pan and spread it over the base of the pan with the fish slice.

5 Dip a half slice of bread into the egg mixture. Coat both sides of the bread and let the mixture soak in a little, but not too much or the bread will become soggy.

6 Place the soaked bread into the pan and cook over a medium heat. There should be room to cook 2–4 halves of bread at a time. When the underneath of the bread is golden brown (lift it up with the fish slice to see), use the fish slice to turn the French toast over to cook on the other side. When the second side is golden brown, lift it out and transfer to a plate. Repeat the process with the rest of the bread, greasing the pan with more butter in between. Keep the French toast in a warm oven while you make the rest.

7 Serve warm, either sprinkled with sugar and cinnamon, or drizzled with maple syrup.

Real Pizza

Serves 6

Ingredients:

Base:

10 g (³/₈ oz) dried yeast*

2 teaspoons sugar

about 300 ml (10 fl oz) warm water
   (not hot)

400 g (14 oz) high grade /strong white
   flour

1 teaspoon salt

4 tablespoons olive oil

extra flour for kneading

extra oil

Topping:

tomato sauce (see page 44)

150 g (6 oz) cheese (Mozzarella or
   Cheddar), sliced or grated

Equipment:

kitchen scales and measures

1 small bowl

1 large bowl

1 sieve

1 wooden spoon

plastic food wrap (cling film)

1 pastry brush

2 oven trays or pizza stones

1 grater or knife

1 rolling pin

Homemade pizza is easy, it just takes some time. This classic recipe topped with tomato and cheese is called 'Margherita'. You can add other toppings of your choice – salami, ham, mushrooms, olives, the list is endless.

1 Place the yeast and the sugar into the small bowl. Stir in 4 tablespoons of the warm water. Leave until it dissolves and becomes frothy – about ten minutes.

2 Sift the flour and salt into the large bowl. Make a hole (called a 'well') in the centre of the flour.

3 Pour in the yeast, olive oil, and most of the remaining warm water. Stir together with the wooden spoon and add more water if the mixture is still dry. The mixture (called the 'dough') should form into a ball and be soft but not wet and sticky.

4 Sprinkle extra flour on a clean bench. Knead the dough on the bench with clean hands – push it down and away from you with one hand, then pull it back towards you. Repeat this action with your other hand. Continue until the dough feels smooth – about 5 minutes. Add extra flour if the dough sticks to the bench.

5 Wash and dry the large bowl, then brush or wipe the insides with a little oil. Put the dough into the bowl and turn it over. Cover with plastic food wrap, also brushed with oil, and leave the bowl in a warm place for the dough to rise. The dough should double in size– it will take about 45 minutes.

6 Heat the oven to 220°C/425°F/Gas mark 7.

7 Sprinkle the oven trays or pizza stones with flour to stop the dough from sticking.

8 Tip the dough onto the floury bench and cut it in half. Roll out two large circles - about 30 cm (12 in) in diameter.

9 Thinly spread the tomato sauce all over each pizza base. Arrange the cheese and any other toppings on the sauce.

10 Bake for about 18 minutes until the cheese is melted and
    the base is crisp. (In a fan-bake oven you can cook both
    pizzas at the same time.)

11 Before serving let the pizza cool for a few minutes so you
    don't burn your mouth.

Note:
*If you use fresh yeast, use twice
much as dried yeast. For this recipe
you would use 20 g (2/3 oz) of
fresh yeast.

Crostini

Ingredients:

1 stick French bread (slightly stale is best)
4–5 tablespoons olive oil

Equipment:

1 chopping board
1 bread knife
1 small bowl
1 tablespoon
1 pastry brush
1 oven tray

Crostini is the Italian name for small slices of crisp bread. They are served with a variety of toppings. Alexandra and Charlotte especially like to spread them with black olive paste. They are also delicious with slices of tomato, cheese, avocado, ham, pâté, tuna, or cooked vegetables, such as caramelised onions and red peppers. This recipe explains how to make the crostini; you can then use the toppings of your choice.

1. Heat the oven to 200°C/400°F/Gas mark 6.
2. Slice the French bread crossways into pieces about 1 cm (½ in) thick.
3. Pour some olive oil into the bowl – start with about 3 tablespoons, and add more if you run out.
4. Spread out the bread slices on the chopping board. Dip the pastry brush in the oil and lightly brush each slice with oil on both sides.
5. Spread out the oiled slices of bread on the oven tray and bake in the oven for about 6 minutes until the bread is golden. Keep watch because the crostini can quickly burn.
6. When the top side is golden, turn them over. If they are too hot to handle, use tongs. Bake until the other side is also golden, for about 2–3 minutes.
7. Allow the crostini to cool, then store in an airtight container until ready to use.

Note:

Crostini will keep in an airtight container for several days, so you can make them in advance.

Guacamole

Ingredients:

2 ripe avocados

juice of 2 limes or 1 lemon

2 tablespoons fresh coriander (cilantro) leaves

1 fresh red chilli (optional)

2 ripe tomatoes (optional)

2 spring onions (scallions) (optional)

salt

corn chips, or straws of raw carrot, red and green bell pepper and other vegetables, for serving

Equipment:

1 small sharp knife

1 chopping board

1 spoon

1 small bowl

1 lemon-squeezer

1 fork

Guacamole is usually eaten as a dip with corn chips or vegetable straws, but it also goes well with plain cooked chicken or potatoes.

1 Cut the avocados in half lengthways and remove the pit (seed). Scoop out the flesh with the spoon, then chop coarsely and place in the small bowl.

2 Squeeze the juice from the limes or lemon using the lemon-squeezer and pour it over the avocado.

3 Finely chop the coriander and add to the avocado.

4 Finely chop the tomato, the white part of the spring onion, and the chilli, if using* and add them to the avocado mixture.

5 Sprinkle over several pinches of salt and stir everything together with the fork. Taste the guacamole and add more salt, if you like.

6 Serve immediately.

*See How To on page 14.

Note:
Make guacamole just before you serve it because avocado goes brown quickly.
We think it tastes best made with all of the optional ingredients, but if you don't like, or don't have, one of them then leave it out. Don't leave out all of the optional ingredients though, because the flavour won't be as good.

Sushi

Makes about 30

Ingredients:

400 g (14 oz) sushi rice (short grain rice)

750 ml (24 fl oz) water

75 ml (2½ fl oz) rice vinegar

pinch of salt

3 teaspoons white (granulated) sugar

5 sheets nori (sushi seaweed wrappers)

Filling:

carrot

red pepper

avocado

cucumber

salmon

cooked chicken

tuna

soy sauce and pickled ginger for
 serving (optional)

Equipment

kitchen scales and measures

1 sieve

1 medium saucepan with lid

1 teaspoon

1 large glass or china bowl

1 spatula

1 small saucepan

1 chopping board

1 sharp knife

1 bamboo sushi rolling mat or
 clean tea-towel

plastic food wrap (cling film)

Sushi is great for packed lunches. Choose whatever filling or combination of fillings you prefer.

Prepare the rice:

1 Cook the rice as described on page 18.

2 Tip the rice into the glass or china bowl and fluff it up by turning it over with a spatula from the bottom of the bowl to the top.

3 Warm the rice vinegar, salt and sugar together in a small saucepan over a low heat. Stir to dissolve the sugar.

4 Slowly pour the vinegar mixture over the cooked rice, turning the rice as you do so to coat all the grains.

5 Leave the rice to cool – it will cool faster if you spread it out on a couple of dinner plates.

Prepare the filling:

1 Peel the carrot, if using. Halve and remove the seeds from the bell pepper, if using.

2 Cut whatever fillings you have chosen into long thin strips.

Assemble the sushi:

1 Place the sushi mat or tea-towel on the bench. Place a nori sheet, rough side facing upwards, on the mat.

2 Spread a large spoonful of rice over the nori sheet, leaving 2 cm (¾ in) clear at the top and lower edges. Press the rice down with the back of the spoon to compact it.

3 Arrange a row of filling(s) on the rice about 3 cm (1¼ in) from the edge closest to you.

4 Carefully roll up the sushi mat, using your fingers to press the filling onto the rice while you use your thumbs to lift up the edge of the sushi mat nearest to you and roll it over the rice. When the edge of the nori sheet meets the rice after the first roll, tuck the nori sheet under. Carefully lift up the edge of the

mat so that it does not get rolled under with the nori sheet, and continue to use the mat to roll the rest of the sushi. Gently squeeze the mat to compact the sushi. Take the roll out of the mat and wrap it in plastic food wrap until you are ready to use it.

5 Repeat with the rest of the rice and nori sheets.

6 To serve, use a sharp knife to slice the sushi roll crossways into 2 cm (¾ in) pieces. Serve sushi with soy sauce and pickled ginger, if you like.

Pan Bagna

Serves 4

Ingredients:

1 stick French bread (a fat stick is best)

1 garlic clove

olive oil

salt

black pepper

Filling: (select some or all of these)

tomatoes

basil leaves

red bell pepper

ham or salami slices

black olives (without pits) or black olive paste

lettuce

hard-boiled eggs

Equipment:

1 chopping board

1 bread knife

plastic food wrap (cling film)

a medium weight, such as a large book, a heavy can or pile of plates

This is really like a slightly compressed filled roll so we call it 'squashed sandwich'. In the south of France, where it comes from, it is called pan bagna (pronounced pan ban yah). Because the bread is weighted down, the filling presses deliciously into the bread, but since the bread is thick it doesn't go horribly soggy. You can leave it in the refrigerator overnight for lunch the next day.

1 Cut the bread stick in half lengthways, so the top crust is one half and the bottom crust is the other half.

2 Peel the garlic and cut in half, then rub it over the cut surface of the bread.

3 Dribble a little bit of olive oil over the cut surface of the bread – not too much or the bread will go soggy.

4 Slice whatever fillings you are using.

5 On the bottom half of the bread stick spread layers of the fillings you have chosen, for example, tomato slices, then basil leaves, red pepper, salami, and black olives.

6 Place the other half of the bread on top and wrap it tightly in plastic food wrap. Place the sandwich on a plate or a tray and place the medium weight on top. Leave the sandwich for about 1 hour.

7 To serve, slice the bread crossways into sections.

Kedgeree

Serves 4

Ingredients:

400 g (14 oz) uncooked long grain rice
  (Basmati rice is especially good)

700 ml (24 fl oz) cold water

4 eggs

1 lemon

450 g (1 lb) smoked fish fillets

fresh parsley, about 1 tablespoon when
  chopped (optional)

60g (2 oz) butter

salt

black pepper

pinch or two of paprika or cayenne
  pepper (optional)

1 lemon, cut into quarters (optional)

Equipment:

1 medium saucepan with lid

kitchen scales and measures

1 sieve

1 saucepan

1 frying pan

1 chopping board

1 sharp knife

1 fish slice

1 fork

1 wooden spoon

1 large serving dish

Kedgeree is a really useful recipe as it can be served for breakfast, lunch or dinner. Plus you can prepare the rice, eggs and fish in advance, so all you need to do when you want to serve the kedgeree is assemble the dish.

1   Cook the rice as described on page 18.

2   Hard boil the eggs as described on page 26 (cook for 5 minutes once the water is simmering).

3   Poach the fish: half fill a frying pan with water and bring it to the boil over a medium heat. Slice the lemon into 1 cm (½ in) slices and add them to the water. Once the water boils, turn the heat to low so that the water hardly has any bubbles on top, then gently lower the fish fillets with their skin side facing upward into the simmering water. Leave the fillets for about 10 minutes to poach, then use a fish slice to lift the fish out of the water, and place on a plate.

4   Chop the parsley leaves, if using.

5   To assemble the kedgeree, peel the skin off the fish fillets and discard. Use a fork to break the fish fillets into chunks, taking out any bones that you see.

6   Peel the eggs, then cut them into quarters.

7   Melt the butter in the frying pan. Add the cooked rice to the pan and stir it around in the butter. Add the fish and parsley, then stir again. Taste the rice on a teaspoon to see if it needs extra flavour. If it does, sprinkle over some salt, black pepper and paprika or cayenne pepper, if using, and stir in.

8   Spoon the rice mixture onto a large serving dish. Arrange the egg quarters over the top and the lemon quarters around the dish and serve.

Pasta with Tomato Sauce

Serves 4

Ingredients:

Tomato Sauce:

2 onions

2 garlic cloves

4 tablespoons olive oil

2 x 400 g (14 oz) cans tomatoes

6 sprigs fresh thyme

6 tablespoons tomato paste/concentrate

extra salt and some black pepper

salt and pepper

about 450 g (1 lb) dried pasta spirals

freshly grated Parmesan or Cheddar
cheese, for serving (optional)

Equipment:

1 chopping board

1 sharp knife

1 large frying pan

1 can opener

1 wooden spoon

1 large saucepan with lid

1 sieve or colander

This is a basic recipe for tomato sauce. It makes a lot so you may not need all of it on the pasta. Try it on pizza bases or with sausages and chicken.

1 Peel and chop the onions and garlic.*

2 Heat the olive oil in a frying pan and gently fry the onion until it is soft but do not let it go brown.

3 Add the garlic and fry for 1 minute more.

4 Open the cans of tomatoes, add them to the pan and chop them with a wooden spoon. Add the sprigs of fresh thyme. Let the mixture simmer for at least 15 minutes.

5 Meanwhile fill a large saucepan with cold water, cover with the lid and bring the water to the boil.

6 Stir the tomato paste/concentrate into the tomato mixture and let the sauce cook gently until quite thick. Stir the sauce occasionally so that it does not stick to the base of the pan.

7 Add the salt to the boiling water. Add the pasta to the water, stir, then let the water boil without the lid until the pasta is cooked. To test if the pasta is cooked, remove a piece from the water and bite it; it should be firm but soft enough to eat. When the pasta is cooked, pour the pasta and water into a colander or sieve over the sink to drain, taking care not to burn yourself.

8 Taste the tomato sauce and add some salt and pepper, if you like.

9 Tip the drained pasta into a large bowl, or back into its cooking saucepan. Spoon some tomato sauce over the pasta, and mix with a wooden spoon so the pasta is coated with sauce.

10 Sprinkle with grated cheese if you like, and serve.

*See How To on pages 14-15.

Note:

You can also add extra ingredients to the basic recipe, for example, fry some bacon pieces or mince with the onion once it is softened, or add some black olives after the sauce is cooked.

Cold Soba Noodles

Serves 4

Ingredients:

4 litres (7 pints) water
400 g (14 oz) soba noodles
2 spring onions (scallions)
1 medium knob fresh ginger
1 sheet nori
light soy sauce

Equipment:

1 large saucepan with lid
1 wooden spoon
1 colander or large sieve
1 large bowl
1 heatproof jug (pitcher)
1 chopping board
1 sharp knife
1 grater
kitchen scissors

To serve:

Divide the noodles between four plates, then sprinkle some nori strips on each pile. Pour some soy sauce (about 1 tablespoon) into four small cups. Place the dishes containing the ginger, spring onions, extra nori and the cooking water on the table to share, along with some spoons.

Soba noodles are made with buckwheat, which is a type of grain. They were one of our favourite dishes when we holidayed in Japan. They taste so much better than they sound!

1 Pour the water into the saucepan and bring it to the boil over a high heat (cover the saucepan so the water will boil faster).

2 When the water is boiling, add the soba noodles slowly, stirring with the wooden spoon as you do so.

3 Allow the noodles to boil gently over a medium heat until they are cooked; this will take about 4 minutes. The noodles are cooked when they are only just soft when you bite them.

4 You need to save the cooking water for the dipping sauce, so place the colander or sieve over the large bowl and carefully pour the noodles and the cooking water into it. Take the colander or sieve out of the bowl, rest it in the sink and run cold water through the noodles. Allow the noodles to drain and set aside. Pour the cooking water into the jug to use later.

5 Wash and dry the spring onions. Slice off the roots and the green part and discard. Finely slice the white part, then place in a small serving dish.

6 Peel the skin off the fresh ginger and discard, then finely grate the ginger and place in a small serving dish.

7 Cut the sheet of nori in half with the scissors, then cut the halves in half lengthways. With the four lengths of nori on top of each other, cut them into thin strips crossways. Place strips in a small serving dish.

To eat:

Add some of the cooking water to the soy sauce, then add some spring onions and ginger. Using chopsticks or a fork, dip a mouthful of noodles into the watery soy sauce and eat.

Tuscan Vegetable Soup

Serves 4-6

Ingredients:

1 leek or onion

2 carrots

2 stalks celery (optional)

2 garlic cloves

4 leaves silverbeet (chard), stalks included

2 rashers (slices) bacon (optional)

3 tablespoons olive oil

1 x 400 g (14 oz) can tomatoes

1.5 litres (2¾ pints) water

1 cup dried pasta, such as macaroni (optional)

2 x 400 g (14 oz) cans cannellini beans

1 teaspoon salt

black pepper

olive oil and grated Parmesan cheese, for serving

Equipment:

1 chopping board

1 sharp knife

1 vegetable peeler

1 large saucepan

1 tablespoon

1 wooden spoon

1 can opener

1 teaspoon

1 sieve

bowls

This soup is so thick it is almost a stew! It can be varied a lot, as you can see by the number of optional ingredients. It is especially good made in advance and reheated (see page 12).

1 Prepare the vegetables, then set aside in bowls:
   – trim the roots off one end of the leek and the dark green part off the other, and discard. Cut the remaining white and pale green part in half lengthways and wash well between the leaves, then slice into half circles. If using onion, chop it.*
   – peel the carrots, trim both ends, cut in half lengthways then in quarter lengthways, then slice crossways about 1 cm (½ in) thick.
   – trim the ends and leaves from the celery, then slice crossways.
   – peel* and chop the garlic.
   – wash the silverbeet, then cut the white stems away from the green leaves. Slice the stems crossways. Cut the leaves into strips crossways.

2 If using bacon, cut off the fat and discard, then cut the meat into about 1 cm (½ in) squares. Use kitchen scissors if it is easier.

3 Gently heat the olive oil in the saucepan. Add the leek/onion and bacon, stir with a wooden spoon and cook gently for 2 minutes until the leek/onion begins to soften.

4 Add the garlic, carrot and celery, stir together, then cook for 5 minutes.

5 Open the can of tomatoes. Add the tomatoes, water and salt to the soup and bring to the boil.

6 If you are adding pasta to the soup, add it once the water is boiling.

7 Add the silverbeet and simmer until the vegetables are almost soft.

8   Meanwhile, open the cans of beans, tip the beans into a sieve and rinse them well under the cold tap.
    Place about half of the beans into the saucepan.

9   Place the rest of the beans into a bowl and squash them with a fork or a wooden spoon, then add the
    squashed beans to the saucepan and stir. They will thicken the soup.

10 Taste the soup, taking care not to burn your tongue. Add more salt, and some black pepper, if you like.

11 Serve the soup warm with some grated parmesan cheese to sprinkle and olive oil to drizzle over the top
    of the soup.

*See How To on pages 14-15.

Risi e Bisi

Serves 4-6

Ingredients:

500 g (1 lb 2 oz) frozen peas

1 onion

2 rashers (slices) bacon (optional)

60 g (2 oz) butter

1.5 litres (2¾ pints) chicken or
   vegetable stock

400 g (14 oz) Italian risotto rice

salt

60 g (2 oz) Parmesan cheese, grated

fresh parsley, 2 tablespoons
   when chopped

black pepper

Equipment:

kitchen scales and measures

1 large plate

1 chopping board

1 sharp knife or kitchen scissors (optional)

1 large saucepan with lid

1 wooden spoon

1 grater

1 tablespoon

Note:

You can use pumpkin instead of peas, except then the recipe would be called 'risi e zucca'. Use about a quarter of a medium pumpkin, peeled and cut into cubes of about 1 cm (½ in). Add the pumpkin in step 4. You may need adult help to cut the pumpkin.

'Risi e bisi' is Italian for 'rice and peas', and much more exciting in flavour than it sounds. It is a very thick soup, like a wet risotto, and Alexandra and Charlotte love it for a filling lunch or a simple dinner.

1 Spread out the frozen peas on the plate and leave to thaw while you begin the preparation.

2 Chop the onion.*

3 Chop the bacon into pieces about 1 cm (½ in) square, if using. Use kitchen scissors if it is easier.

4 Melt the butter in the saucepan. Add the onion and bacon, then gently fry until the onion is soft and golden, stirring occasionally.

5 Add the stock to the saucepan and bring to the boil over a medium heat.

6 Tip the rice into the stock, add ½ teaspoon salt, place the lid on the saucepan, and simmer for 10 minutes. Stir occasionally during the cooking.

7 While the rice is cooking, grate the Parmesan and chop the parsley.

8 When the rice is cooked but still firm when you bite it, stir in the peas, then cover and cook for another 5 minutes.

9 Take the saucepan off the heat and stir in the Parmesan, chopped parsley and some pepper. Place the lid back on and let it rest for about 4 minutes. Taste the rice and add more salt and pepper if you like. Serve in soup bowls.

*See How To on page 15.

Bubble and Squeak

Ingredients:

1 onion

cooked potatoes (mashed, roasted or boiled)

cooked cabbage or Brussels sprouts

about 60 g (2 oz) butter

salt

black pepper

Equipment:

1 chopping board

1 sharp knife

1 medium frying pan

1 fish slice

Note:

Don't worry if the bubble and squeak falls apart when you turn it over or dish it up – it will still taste delicious. Although cabbage is traditional in bubble and squeak, you could use other cooked vegetables with the potato.

This is usually made with leftovers; however, it is so delicious it is worth cooking extra potato and cabbage just to have enough the next day to make bubble and squeak. The amounts of potato and cabbage do not have to be exact; you can have more potato than cabbage or equal amounts of each.

1 Peel and chop the onion.*

2 Chop the potatoes, unless they are already mashed, into chunks about 1 cm (½ in) square. Slice the Brussels sprouts, if using.

3 Melt half the butter in the frying pan over a medium heat, add the onion and cook until it is soft.

4 Add the potato and cabbage/Brussels sprouts, salt and pepper, and mix with the onion. Press the mixture down so that it sticks together, then cook over a medium heat until the bubble and squeak is brown underneath (about 15 minutes).

5 Divide the bubble and squeak into quarters with a knife, then turn each quarter over with a fish slice to brown the other side. As you turn them over add the rest of the butter to the pan.

6 Serve warm.

*See How To on page 15.

Dhal

Serves 4-6

Ingredients:

340 g (12 oz) split red lentils

1 litre (1¾ pints) cold water

3 medium onions

3 tablespoons vegetable oil

3 garlic cloves

1 medium knob fresh ginger
  (¾ teaspoon when grated)

1 fresh red chilli or ½ teaspoon
  chilli powder (optional)

¾ teaspoon turmeric

¾ teaspoon ground cumin seeds

½ teaspoon ground coriander seeds

2 tablespoons cold water

salt

about 2 tablespoons lemon juice

fresh coriander (cilantro) leaves (optional)

Equipment:

kitchen scales and measures

1 sieve

1 large saucepan with lid

1 chopping board

1 knife

1 frying pan

1 grater

1 tablespoon

measuring spoons

Dhal is an Indian dish usually served with boiled rice (see page 18). We also like to eat it with roti, a type of Indian bread that you can find in most supermarkets.

1 Place the lentils in the sieve and rinse them well under cold running water. Place them in the saucepan and add the cold water.

2 Bring the lentils to the boil (without the lid) over a medium heat, scooping off any scum that collects on the top with a spoon.

3 Meanwhile, chop 1½ onions* and add to the lentils when they are boiling. Cover the saucepan with the lid, lower the heat and allow the lentils to simmer gently for about 30 minutes until they are soft.

4 While the lentils are simmering, slice the remaining 1½ onions into semi-circles.

5 Heat the oil gently in the frying pan and cook the semi-circles of onion slowly until they are soft and brown, then remove them from the pan and set aside.

6 Peel* and chop the garlic. Peel and grate the ginger. If using fresh chilli, slice it.* Add the garlic, ginger, chilli or chilli powder, turmeric, cumin and ground coriander to the frying pan and cook for 2 minutes, stirring.

7 Add the cold water to the pan and stir, then add the water and spices to the saucepan of lentils. Add ½ teaspoon of salt and stir.

8 Simmer the lentils gently, with the lid off, until they are like thin porridge.

9 Taste the lentils and add more salt, if you like. Stir in the lemon juice.

10 Chop coriander leaves, if using.

11 To serve, dish the lentils into a bowl and spread the browned onion slices on top. Scatter chopped
    coriander leaves over the lentils, if using.

*See How To on pages 14-15.

Macaroni Cheese

Serves 6-8

Ingredients:

Cheese sauce:
150 g (5¼ oz) Cheddar cheese

40 g (1½ oz) butter

25 g (⁷/₈ oz) plain white flour

400 mls (14 fl oz) milk (whole (full fat milk) is best)

salt

pepper

1 pinch grated nutmeg (optional)

400 g (14 oz) macaroni

1 teaspoon salt

Topping (optional):
80 g (2¾) extra grated Cheddar cheese

1 tablespoon dried breadcrumbs

Equipment:
kitchen scales and measures

1 large saucepan

1 medium-sized saucepan

1 wooden spoon

1 chopping board

1 grater

1 sieve or colander

1 ovenproof dish (optional)

'Mac n' Cheese' was a favourite dish when I was a child and I still love it. The cheese sauce can be used for many other recipes such as Poached Chicken (page 62).

1 Three-quarters fill the large saucepan with cold water, cover, and bring the water to the boil over a high heat. To bake the macaroni cheese (see step 10), heat the oven to 180°C /350°F/Gas mark 4.

2 When the water is boiling, add the salt and the macaroni. Stir a couple of times with the wooden spoon so it does not stick together.

3 Boil the macaroni uncovered until it is just cooked, about 12 minutes. To test, remove a piece with a spoon and bite it; it should be firm but still soft enough to eat.

4 Grate the cheese for the sauce.

5 Make the cheese sauce while the macaroni is cooking. Melt the butter in the medium-sized saucepan over a medium heat. Stir in the flour with a wooden spoon and cook for about 2 minutes until it turns pale. Remove from heat. (This butter and flour mixture is called a 'roux').

6 Pour in 2 tablespoons of milk and stir until it is mixed evenly. Repeat with 2 more tablespoons of milk. At first it will go very thick but continue to add the milk gradually, stirring until the roux is smooth and runny. (By stirring in the milk a little at a time, you will avoid lumps.) When all of the milk is added, put the saucepan back on the heat and stir continuously until it begins to boil.

7 Lower the heat. Add the grated cheese and stir until melted through the sauce. Remove from heat.

8 Taste the sauce and add some salt, pepper and nutmeg, if you like.

9 Drain the cooked macaroni in a colander or sieve over the sink, taking care not to burn yourself. Tip it back into the saucepan. Pour over the cheese sauce and mix well. The macaroni cheese is now ready to eat. If you want to make it extra-cheesy, continue to step 10 below.

10 Tip the macaroni cheese into an ovenproof dish. Spread over extra grated cheese and a light sprinkling of dried bread crumbs and bake in the oven for about 10 minutes. Serve.

Note:
This recipe can be made in advance and reheated when required – as described in step 10

Spanakopita

Serves 4

Ingredients:

1 onion

about 4 tablespoons olive oil

about 400 g (14 oz) fresh spinach or
    350 g (12 oz) frozen spinach

250 g (9 oz) plain cottage cheese

200 g (7 oz) feta cheese

fresh parsley, 1½ teaspoons when
    chopped (optional)

black pepper

few pinches of ground nutmeg

4–5 sheets filo pastry

Equipment:

kitchen scales and measures

1 sharp knife

1 chopping board

1 frying pan

1 large saucepan with lid

1 sieve

1 wooden spoon

1 large bowl

1 ovenproof dish, 1 litre (1¾ pints)
capacity

1 small dish

1 pastry brush

You don't have to like spinach to enjoy this Greek dish — the cheeses make it really delicious.

1 Heat the oven to 180°C/350°F/Gas mark 4.

2 Chop the onion.* Gently heat 1 tablespoon of olive oil in a frying pan, and cook the onion until soft, but not brown.

3 Meanwhile prepare the spinach. For fresh spinach, fill the sink with about 5 cm (2 in) of cold water, add the spinach and swish it around to wash. Remove the spinach from the sink, empty the sink, and repeat the process. Pull the spinach leaves off the stems. Place the leaves into a large saucepan (discard the stems), cover with the lid and cook until the spinach is just wilted (soft and limp). For frozen spinach, cook according to the instructions on the packet. When the spinach is cooked, drain very well in a sieve, pressing the water out with a wooden spoon. Chop the drained spinach on a board with a knife.

4 Place the spinach in a large bowl. Add the cooked onion, and the cottage cheese.

5 Drain the water from the feta, chop into pieces about 1 cm (½ in) square, and add to the spinach mixture.

6 Chop the parsley and add to the mixture, if using. Add the black pepper and nutmeg, then stir until mixed.

7 Place the mixture in the ovenproof dish.

8 Remove the filo sheets from their packet and place them flat in a pile on top of each other. (Immediately wrap up the rest of the filo pastry so that it won't dry out.) Pour a little olive oil into a small dish and brush a sheet of pastry on one side with oil. Scrunch up the pastry as if you were loosely screwing up paper and place it, oily side up, on top of the spinach mixture. Repeat this process 3–4 times. The mixture should be completely covered with scrunched-up pastry.

9 Place the dish in the oven and bake for about 15–20 minutes until the pastry is golden and crisp. Serve warm.

*See How To on page 15.

Gado-Gado Salad

Serves 4

Ingredients:

Peanut Sauce:

1 tablespoon vegetable oil
1 onion
1 clove of garlic
½ teaspoon salt
½ teaspoon chilli powder or 1 fresh chilli
  (optional)
¼ teaspoon brown sugar
250 ml (8.7 fl oz) cold water
150 g (5 oz) crunchy peanut butter
juice ½ lemon

Salad:

2 eggs
2 medium potatoes
2 handfuls round green beans
4 florets cauliflower
1 carrot
¼ cucumber
½ red pepper
60 g (2 oz) bean sprouts
1 medium wedge of cabbage or a few
  leaves iceberg lettuce
salt

Equipment:

Kitchen scales and measures
1 sharp knife
1 chopping board
1 lemon squeezer
1 frying pan
1 wooden spoon
2 saucepans
1 medium-sized bowl
1 slotted spoon
sieve

Gado-gado, an Indonesian salad of crunchy vegetables topped with spicy peanut sauce, is a delicious way to eat vegetables. It's one of Charlotte's all-time favourite dishes. You don't have to use all the vegetables — just use the salad ingredients you like. The peanut sauce makes a great topping for other recipes too!

Peanut Sauce:

1 Finely chop the onion. Peel* and crush or chop the garlic. Slice the chilli*, if using. Squeeze the lemon juice*.

2 Heat the oil in the frying pan and gently fry the onion, stirring occasionally until it is soft.

3 Add the garlic to the browned onion and fry for about 1 minute. Add the chilli or chilli powder, if using.

4 Stir in the peanut butter, water, sugar and salt. Let the mixture simmer until it thickens, stirring occasionally.

5 Stir in the lemon juice. Taste the sauce and add more salt if you like.

Salad:

1 Hard-boil the eggs* (about 5 minutes).

2 Pour water into a saucepan and bring it to the boil. Fill a bowl with cold water.

3 Prepare the vegetables to be cooked:
   – peel or scrub the potatoes, and cut them into quarters.
   – peel the carrot and cut it into 'straws' about 4 cm (1½ in) long.
   – cut the cauliflower into small even-sized florets.
   – trim the tops of the beans.

4 Add ¼ of a teaspoon of salt to the boiling water. Cook the potatoes in the water.

5 If using carrots, cauliflower and/or beans, cook one type of vegetable at a time with the potatoes. When the vegetables

are softened but still firm when poked with a sharp knife, remove them with a slotted spoon and place in
the bowl of cold water. Drain the vegetables in a sieve and put them on a plate while the next vegetable
is cooking, then put more water in the bowl. When the potatoes are cooked right through, remove them
from the pot and leave to cool.

7 Prepare the raw vegetables:
   - rinse the lettuce or cabbage in cold water, then dry (either pat dry with a clean tea towel or paper
     towel, or spin in a lettuce spinner). If using cabbage, slice finely. If using lettuce, tear into small pieces.
   - rinse the bean sprouts in a sieve.
   - rinse and dry the cucumber and/ or red pepper and remove seeds from the red pepper. Finely slice.

Assemble the salad:

1. Peel the eggs and cut into quarters. Cut the potato quarters into chunks.
2. On a large serving plate or salad bowl, spread out the lettuce or cabbage.
3. Spread the cucumber and/or red pepper on top, then scatter the cauliflower, carrots, beans and potato,
   followed by the egg and the bean sprouts.
4. Spoon the sauce over the salad. Serve.

*see How to on pages 14-16

Poached Chicken Breasts

Serves 4

Ingredients:

4 chicken breasts without skin

water

1 sprig of fresh parsley

1 sprig of fresh thyme

1 bay leaf

6 black peppercorns

Equipment:

I large saucepan

1 slotted spoon

Note:
Strain the poaching water through a sieve into a large bowl. Cool, then cover and refrigerate. When cold, scrape off any fat that has set on the surface.

This is a really useful recipe for cooking chicken because it is quick and simple, and the meat is always moist. It can be served with tomato sauce (page 44), peanut sauce (page 60), or cheese sauce (page 56), or in a sandwich or soup. It's really two recipes in one because the poaching water can be saved as chicken stock for soup.

1 Half fill the saucepan with cold water. Add the herbs and peppercorns and put on a medium heat to bring the water to the boil.

2 Add the chicken breasts, carefully. The water should just cover the chicken. Lower the heat so that the surface of the water almost bubbles but not quite. (This is called 'poaching'.) Poach the chicken for 15–20 minutes.

3 Remove the cooked chicken from the water with a slotted spoon. (To check if the chicken is properly cooked, cut one chicken breast in half. If it is not completely white all the way through return all the meat to the poaching water and cook longer.) Serve with your chosen sauce.

Variation
Chicken Noodle Soup

Boil the poaching water until it has reduced to half of the original amount — you will need about 1 litre (35 fl oz). Add 100g (3 oz) spaghetti to the chicken stock and simmer until it is soft. Add 1 tablespoon of chopped fresh parsley, salt and black pepper, and some pieces of cooked poached chicken.

Roast Chicken

Ingredients:

1 whole chicken (about 1.4 kg
  (3¼ lb)

1 lemon

1 tablespoon olive oil

1 clove garlic (optional)

4–8 sprigs fresh thyme

salt

black pepper

250 ml (8 fl oz) water

Equipment:

1 roasting dish just big enough to
  hold the chicken

1 chopping board

1 sharp knife

1 tablespoon

aluminium foil

Roast chicken is a family favourite. This version with lemon is especially delicious. You need to begin this recipe about 1¾ hours before you want to eat it.

1 Heat the oven to 200°C/400°F/Gas mark 6.

2 Unwrap the chicken. If there is a bag of giblets in the cavity (the middle of the chicken), remove them and discard. Rinse the chicken including the cavity under the cold tap.

3 Place the chicken in the roasting dish, with the breast side facing upward.

4 Slice the lemon into slices about 0.5 cm/¼ in thick. Peel* and slice the garlic, if using.

5 Place half of the lemon slices, the garlic slices and 2–4 sprigs of thyme into the cavity.

6 Pour the olive oil over the skin of the chicken and rub it in with your hands, then wash your hands well.

7 Sprinkle salt and pepper over the chicken, then place the rest of the thyme on top of the chicken and the remaining lemon slices on top of the thyme. Pour the water around the edge of the chicken.

8 Put the chicken into the oven, noting the time. Make sure you wash your hands, the knife, the chopping board, and anything else that has been in contact with the raw chicken in warm soapy water and dry them well.

9 After about 30 minutes of cooking, remove the roasting dish from the oven and scoop up the juices in the dish with a spoon and pour them over the top of the chicken. This is called basting and it keeps the chicken moist. Return the roasting dish to the oven. Do this again in 15 minutes' time, and again 15 minutes later. At this point remove the lemon slices from the top of the chicken. If the chicken starts to look too brown cover it with some aluminium foil.

10 When the chicken has been in the oven for 1¼ hours, test to see if it is cooked by poking the tip of a sharp knife into a thigh. If the juices run out clear, it is cooked; if the juices are pink, it will need another 10 minutes or so until it is cooked. It is very important that the chicken is properly cooked.

11 When the chicken is cooked, lift the roasting dish out of the oven, transfer the chicken to a serving plate and leave to rest in a warm place for 15 minutes before carving.

*See How To on page 14.

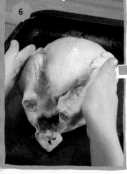

Chicken Nibbles

Serves 4

Ingredients:
Marinade:

1 garlic clove

1 lemon

2 tablespoons liquid honey

2 tablespoons soy sauce

40 chicken nibbles/about 2 kg (4½ lb)

Equipment:

1 chopping board

1 sharp knife

1 lemon-squeezer

1 tablespoon

1 large bowl and plastic food wrap
  (cling film) or 1 large clean plastic
  bag

1 roasting dish

1 large spoon or kitchen tongs

1 ovenproof serving dish

Note:

You can marinate the chicken in a bowl or a dish, but the easiest way to do it is to put the marinade and chicken into a clean, large plastic bag (a ziplock bag is best). You can mix the marinade in the bag, or mix it in a jug then pour it in. Just in case the bag gets a hole in it sit the whole thing in a bowl.

Chicken nibbles are small pieces of chicken wing on the bone. They are great finger food and are always popular when we serve them at parties. The recipe itself is quick to prepare, but you need to begin at least 3 hours before you want to eat the nibbles so they can absorb the delicious flavours of the marinade. The marinade is the same as for the spare ribs on page 68, but chicken nibbles are cooked differently.

1 Make the marinade: Peel* and crush or chop the garlic. Squeeze the juice from the lemon.* Mix the honey, soy sauce, garlic and lemon juice together either in a bowl or in a large plastic bag.

2 Place the chicken nibbles in the marinade. If using a bowl, stir the chicken nibbles, turning them over and over in the marinade until they are well coated, then cover with plastic food wrap. If using a plastic bag, close it, then gently squish the bag so that the chicken is coated.

3 Place the chicken in the bottom of the refrigerator for a least 1 hour. It can stay there for up to several hours.

4 When ready to cook the nibbles, heat the oven to 180°C/350°F/Gas mark 4.

5 When the oven is hot, tip the chicken nibbles and the marinade into the roasting dish, spreading the chicken out in an even layer. Place the dish in the oven and bake for 1¼ hours. During the cooking use a clean spoon or tongs to turn the chicken nibbles over in the marinade so that they stay moist and cook evenly. Repeat this about 3 times.

6 When the nibbles are cooked, switch off the oven, remove the roasting dish from the oven and use a clean spoon or tongs to lift them out of the marinade and transfer to an ovenproof serving dish. Place the serving dish in the oven for 15 minutes.

7 Serve warm.

*See How To on pages 14 and 16.

Spare Ribs

Serves 4

Ingredients:

Marinade:

1 garlic clove

1 lemon

2 tablespoons liquid honey

2 tablespoons soy sauce

1.25 kg (2¾ lbs) spare ribs (skinned pork belly pieces), cut into separate pieces

Equipment:

1 chopping board

1 sharp knife

1 lemon-squeezer

1 tablespoon

1 large bowl and plastic food wrap (cling film) or 1 large clean plastic bag

1 roasting dish

aluminium foil

1 large spoon or kitchen tongs

Spare ribs are fun to gnaw on – and eating them with your fingers is part of the pleasure. The recipe itself is quick to prepare but you need to begin at least 3 hours before you want to eat the ribs. The marinade is the same as for the chicken nibbles on page 66, but they are cooked a little differently.

The method is the same for steps 1, 2, and 3 of the chicken nibbles on page 66.

4   When you are ready to cook the spare ribs, heat the oven to 180°C/350°F/Gas mark 4.

5   When the oven is hot, tip the ribs and the marinade into the roasting dish, spreading the ribs out in an even layer. Cover the top of the roasting dish with aluminium foil, scrunching it over the top edges of the dish so that everything is completely covered. Place the dish in the oven and bake for 45 minutes. After 45 minutes, remove the dish from the oven, take off the foil, then place the dish back into the oven for another 45 minutes. During this time use a spoon or tongs to turn the ribs over in the marinade so that they stay moist and cook evenly. Repeat this several times. Eventually the ribs will darken and become shiny.

6   When the ribs are cooked, remove the dish from the oven and use clean tongs or a spoon to lift the ribs out of the roasting dish and arrange on a serving dish. Serve warm.

Baked Beans with Sausages

Serves 4

Ingredients:

3 x 400 g (14 oz) cans white beans
   (haricot or cannellini)

1 onion

4 cloves garlic

1 x 400 g (14 oz) can tomatoes

3 tablespoons tomato paste/concentrate

250 ml (8 fl oz) water

salt

black pepper

1 bay leaf

2 sprigs fresh thyme or a pinch of
   dried thyme

2 sprigs fresh parsley

4–8 sausages (chorizo or regular pork)

Equipment:

1 can opener

1 sieve

1 large casserole dish with lid

1 chopping board

1 sharp knife

1 spoon

These baked beans are much nicer than the canned variety. The choice of sausage is up to you: if you find chorizo too spicy, use regular pork sausages; or if you like a little bit of spice, use half chorizo and half regular sausages; and if you like rather spicy use all chorizo.

1 Heat the oven to 180°C/350°F/Gas mark 4.

2 Open the cans of beans, tip them into a sieve and rinse under the cold tap. Place them in the casserole dish.

3 Chop the onion*, and add to the casserole.

4 Peel the garlic* and add whole to the casserole.

5 Open the can of tomatoes, and add them to the casserole with the tomato paste/concentrate and water.

6 Add salt, pepper, the bay leaf, thyme and parsley to the casserole.

7 Slice the chorizo sausages, if using, into pieces about 2 cm (¾ in) long and add to the casserole.

8 Stir everything so that it is mixed. If using pork sausages, place them on top of the other ingredients.

9 Put the lid on the casserole dish and place in the centre of the oven. Bake for about 1½ hours; half way through the cooking time stir and check the bean mixture. If it looks too dry add a little more water.

10 Serve.

*See How To on pages 14-15.

Moroccan Lamb

Serve 5-6

Ingredients:

1–1.25 kg (2¼–2¾ lb) boned shoulder of lamb

2 medium onions

15g (½ oz) butter

2 tablespoons oil

½ teaspoon black pepper

1 teaspoon ground ginger

1 teaspoon ground cumin

½ tablespoon ground cinnamon

½ teaspoon salt

about 400 ml (14 fl oz) water

175 g (6 oz) dried apricots

225 g (9 oz) prunes

1 cinnamon stick

2 long strips lemon rind

3 tablespoons honey

Couscous for 4

175 g (6 oz) couscous

250 ml (8 fl oz) boiling water

15g (½ oz) butter

¼ teaspoon salt

Equipment:

1 chopping board

1 sharp knife

1 casserole dish with lid that can cook on the stove top and in the oven

measuring spoons

kitchen scales and measures

You can make this recipe with prunes and dried apricots or just prunes or just dried apricots – whatever you prefer. For prunes alone use 450 g (1 lb); for apricots alone use 350 g (12 oz).

1 Trim the visible fat off the lamb, then cut the meat into 4 cm (1¾ in) cubes.

2 Chop the onions.✱

3 Melt the butter in the casserole over a medium heat, then take it off the heat and add the oil, pepper, ginger, cumin, ground cinnamon, salt and lamb cubes. Stir them around so that the lamb is coated with the spices.

4 Return the casserole to the stove top and cook the lamb mixture over a medium heat for about 3 minutes, while stirring.

5 Add the chopped onion and enough water to just cover the mixture.

6 Put the lid on the casserole, but leave a gap for steam to escape. Bring the mixture to the boil, then lower the heat and simmer gently for 1 hour.

7 After 1 hour, add the apricots and/or prunes, cinnamon stick, lemon zest and honey and stir into the lamb mixture.

8 Simmer the casserole uncovered for about 30 minutes. The sauce will become thicker and coat the meat. If it gets too thick and you think it is going to burn, add a little more water.

9 Serve with couscous.

*See How To on page 15.

Couscous

Couscous is tiny pellets of wheat and is usually served instead of potatoes or rice.

Equipment:

Couscous

1 medium bowl

1 tablespoon

kitchen scales and measures

1 fork

1 Place the couscous in the bowl.

2 Stir in 250 ml (8 fl oz) of boiling water, the butter in small lumps, and salt. Leave the couscous to absorb all the water – this will take about 5 minutes.

3 When all of the water is absorbed, stir the couscous again with a fork. Taste the couscous – if it is firm, then stir in some more boiling water and leave to absorb. Taste it again, and if necessary add more water, and/or more salt.

Roast Potatoes or Wedges

Serves 4

Ingredients:

4–5 medium potatoes (about 900 g/2 lbs)
salt
4 tablespoons oil

Equipment:

1 knife or vegetable peeler
1 chopping board
1 medium saucepan with lid
1 sieve
1 tablespoon
1 roasting dish

The only difference between roast potatoes and wedges is their shape. You can cook them both by the same method. Crisp and golden on the outside and soft and fluffy on the inside, they are so scrumptious you will need to make plenty.

1 Heat the oven to 200°C/400°F/Gas mark 6.

2 Peel the potatoes and cut them into chunks approximately 5 cm (2 in) in size or into wedge shapes.

3 Place the potatoes in the saucepan and add just enough cold water to cover. Add ¼ teaspoon salt and bring to the boil over a medium heat. Simmer the potatoes until they are half cooked, so that when a sharp knife is inserted into one, the outside will be soft, but the centre will be hard.

4 Drain the potatoes into the sieve over the sink. Gently shake the potatoes around in the sieve to roughen the outsides.

5 Pour the oil into the roasting dish and warm it in the hot oven.

6 Remove the dish from the oven and gently place the potatoes in the oil. Use a spoon to roll them over in the oil so that each piece of potato is thoroughly coated in oil. Take care that the hot oil doesn't splash you or your clothes.

7 Return the roasting dish to the oven, and roast the potatoes for about 45 minutes to 1 hour, until they are golden and crisp on the outside and soft in the centre. There is no need to turn them during the roasting.

8 Remove the dish from the oven, sprinkle the cooked potatoes with salt and serve warm.

Note:

If you are roasting potatoes at the same time as chicken, you can either roast the chicken in one small dish and the potatoes in another if there is enough room in the oven, or you can use one larger dish and put the oil-coated potatoes around the chicken. Then when the chicken is cooked and removed from the oven to rest, transfer the potatoes to a clean ovenproof dish and put them back in the oven to crisp up.

Honeyed Carrots

Serves 4

Ingredients:
600 g (1 lb 6 oz) carrots

water

salt

75 g (2½ oz) butter

3 tablespoons honey

Equipment:
1 vegetable peeler

1 knife

1 chopping board

1 medium saucepan with lid

1 colander or sieve

1 frying pan

1 tablespoon

If you like sweet foods, you are bound to love these carrots. They are super sweet! Serve them with simple, savoury dishes, such as roast meat, or grilled (broiled) sausages, for a contrast.

1 Peel the carrots, then slice them diagonally crossways about 0.5 cm (¼ in) thick.

2 Place the carrots in a saucepan, add enough water to just cover, and a couple of pinches of salt. Bring the carrots to the boil over a medium heat, then simmer them until they are nearly cooked; they will still be quite firm when you pierce one with a sharp knife.

3 Drain the carrots into a colander or sieve over the sink.

4 Melt the butter in a frying pan, then add the honey.

5 Add the almost-cooked carrots to the pan and gently stir them in the butter and honey mixture until they are coated.

6 Continue to cook the carrots for about 20 minutes over a low heat, turning them over occasionally, until they are brown and shiny.

7 Serve.

Note:
You can use this recipe to transform other everyday vegetables into a special dish. Parsnips, and even little turnips and kumara (sweet potato) taste delicious cooked in this way.

Simple Cauliflower or Broccoli Cheese

Ingredients:

1 head broccoli or 1 cauliflower

salt

4 tablespoons grated (shredded)
Cheddar cheese

Equipment:

1 medium saucepan

1 sharp knife

1 chopping board

1 colander or sieve

1 grater

1 serving dish

Cauliflower and broccoli go really well with cheese.

1 Half-fill a saucepan with water and bring to the boil over a medium heat.

2 Cut off as many florets of broccoli or cauliflower as you need and wash them.

3 Put ¼ teaspoon salt in the boiling water and add the broccoli or cauliflower florets. Simmer until they are just tender – test by piercing the stalk with a sharp knife.

4 Drain in a colander or sieve over the sink.

5 Place the broccoli or cauliflower in a serving dish and sprinkle the grated cheese evenly over the top. The cheese will melt because the vegetable is hot.

6 Serve immediately.

Ten-Minute Noodles

Serves 4

Ingredients:

400 g (14 oz) rice sticks or 600 g
(1 lb 6 oz) udon noodles

1 x 400 g (14 oz) can coconut cream

3 tablespoons fish sauce

3 tablespoons lime or lemon juice

2.5 cm (1 in) knob fresh ginger

1 fresh red chilli* or ¼ teaspoon chilli
flakes (optional)

Kaffir lime leaf (optional)

1 spring onion (scallion), or chives
(optional)

fresh coriander (cilantro) leaves (optional)

Equipment:

1 large bowl

1 medium-sized saucepan

1 tablespoon

1 sharp knife

1 can-opener

1 colander or large sieve

kitchen scissors

Note:
You can also add extra ingredients to the basic recipe. For example, add some bok choy, sliced mushrooms, red pepper or poached chicken. Or you could add some washed bean sprouts with the spring onion (scallion).

This basic recipe for Thai-flavoured noodles is perfect for a quick tasty snack. You can add extras to make it into a full meal.

1 Place the rice sticks or noodles in the large bowl and cover with boiling water (from a kettle). Set aside.

2 Open the can of coconut cream and pour into the saucepan. Add the fish sauce and lime or lemon juice.

3 Prepare the other seasonings and add them to the coconut cream:
   - peel the skin off the fresh ginger and discard, then finely slice the ginger with the sharp knife.
   - slice the fresh chilli, if using.
   - tear the kaffir lime leaves into pieces, if using.

4 Gently bring coconut cream to the boil, and simmer for a minute. Taste and add more fish sauce or juice, if you like.

5 Wash and dry the spring onion (scallion). Slice off the hairy roots and the green part and discard. Finely slice the white part. If using chives, cut with scissors into small pieces. Wash and dry the coriander leaves, if using.

6 Drain the noodles in a sieve or colander over the sink. Share noodles among serving bowls. Spoon over the coconut cream. Sprinkle over the spring onions (scallions) or chives and coriander leaves.

*See how to on page 14.

Variation:
Instead of coconut cream, serve the noodles with peanut sauce (page 60).

Strawberry Ice Cream

Serve 6-8

Ingredients:

about 300 g (10½ oz) strawberries

1 tablespoon lemon juice

3 egg yolks

115 g (4 oz) icing (confectioners') sugar

250 ml (8 fl oz) double (heavy) cream

Equipment:

1 loaf or cake tin (pan), 1 litre (1¾ pints) capacity

plastic food wrap (cling film)

paper towel

kitchen scales and measures

1 small sharp knife

2 medium bowls

1 fork or blender

1 large bowl

1 lemon-squeezer

1 sieve

1 eggbeater

1 spatula

1 large metal spoon

This is actually what Italians call 'semifreddo', which means 'semi-frozen'. It is delicious served on its own, or with fresh strawberries, or with Chocolate Sauce (see page 96). Use really ripe strawberries – they have the most flavour and are easier to pulp.

1 Line the container in which you will freeze the ice cream with a large sheet of plastic food wrap. It should come up the sides and hang over the edges.

2 To prepare the strawberries, wipe with a damp paper towel, then cut off the green tops. Chop the berries into little pieces and place in one of the medium bowls. Pulp the berries by mashing them with a fork against the side of the bowl until runny, or by whizzing them with a blender.

3 Stir the lemon juice into the pulp.

4 Separate the eggs.* Place the egg yolks into the large bowl (save the egg whites for another recipe).

5 Sift the icing sugar and add to the egg yolks and beat until the mixture becomes thick and a paler colour.

6 Pour the cream into another bowl and, using the eggbeater, whip the cream until it is thick.

7 Using the spatula, scrape the whipped cream and the strawberry pulp into the beaten egg yolks and fold all ingredients gently together with the large metal spoon.*

8 Spoon the mixture into the prepared container. Cover the container with more plastic food wrap and carefully place in the freezer for about 7 hours.

9 To serve, remove the plastic food wrap from the top and turn the container upside down onto a plate. Lift off the container, then peel off the food wrap that lined the ice cream. Slice.

*See How To on page 16.

Rice Pudding

Serves 4

Ingredients:

60g (2 oz) short grain rice

1 tablespoon caster (superfine) sugar

570–600 ml (1 pint) whole (full fat) milk

2 drops vanilla extract

3 pinches of grated nutmeg

Equipment:

kitchen scales and measures

1 tablespoon

1 ovenproof dish, 1 litre (1¾ pints) capacity

1 oven tray

Note:

The grains of short grain rice are quite round. Types of short grain rice include sushi rice and Arborio rice. Although short grain rice is best, this recipe also works with medium grain rice.

This is another of my family's favourite puddings, so we make lots by doubling the recipe – and still there is rarely any left over. It's really simple to make, but you have to begin several hours before you want to eat it. Although rice pudding is actually a pudding, it has all the ingredients of a breakfast – a cereal grain, lots of milk and a little sugar – so we have included here a great way to make it overnight ready to eat in the morning.

1 Heat the oven to 120°C/250°F/Gas mark ½.

2 Place the rice and sugar in the ovenproof dish.

3 Pour over the milk, add the vanilla essence and sprinkle with the nutmeg. Gently stir everything together.

4 Place the dish on an oven tray in the oven and bake for about 3 hours. The pudding will develop a brown skin on top and be creamy and soft underneath.

5 Serve as is, or with stewed fruit or a dollop of jam.

Overnight version:

1 Heat the oven to its lowest setting.

2 Prepare the rice pudding exactly the same way as the recipe above.

3 Place the pudding in the oven before you go to bed and leave it to bake overnight. It will not burn as the oven is very low.

Fresh Fruit Salad

Serves 4

Mixed Fruit Salad

1 orange

1 banana

1 apple

10 strawberries

20 grapes/ or blueberries

2 kiwi fruit

Golden/Red Fruit Salad

10 strawberries

1 red-skinned apple

20 red/ black grapes

¼ rock melon (cantaloupe)

¼ pineapple

2 golden kiwifruit

1 orange

Green Fruit Salad

1 green-skinned apple

20 green grapes

2 green kiwifruit

1 banana

¼ honeydew melon

1 pear

Equipment:

1 chopping board

1 knife

1 spoon

1 medium-sized bowl

Charlotte loves fresh fruit but she laughed when I suggested a recipe for fresh fruit salad. "You just cut up fresh fruit", she said. Of course, she's right. Either peel the fruit, or wash and dry the fruit that will not be peeled, then cut it into even bite-sized pieces. Use any combination of fruit available in season that you fancy. Below are some suggestions. Some fruits, such as bananas, apples and pears go brown after they are cut so add them to the salad at the last minute.

Serve on its own or with thick yoghurt, ice cream, or cream.

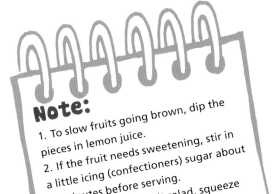

Note:

1. To slow fruits going brown, dip the pieces in lemon juice.
2. If the fruit needs sweetening, stir in a little icing (confectioners) sugar about 15 minutes before serving.
3. To make a juicy fruit salad, squeeze an orange* and pour the juice over the fruit. Some icing sugar (confectioners) sugar can be added to make a thicker, sweeter syrup.

Apple Crumble

Ingredients:

Stewed apples:

900 g (2 lbs) cooking apples

40 g (1¼ oz) butter

2 tablespoons sugar

1 lemon

Crumble:

175 g (6 oz) plain (all-purpose) flour

2 pinches of ground cinnamon or
  ginger (optional)

115 g (4 oz) butter

60g (2 oz) sugar (white or brown)

milk, cream, vanilla ice cream, or
  plain yogurt for serving

Equipment:

1 vegetable peeler

1 chopping board

1 sharp knife

saucepan and lid

kitchen scales and measures

1 medium mixing bowl

1 knife

1 grater

1 ovenproof dish, 1 litre (1¾ pints)
  capacity

1 oven tray

Apple Crumble is a very popular pudding — we make it often. You can use this topping on other stewed fruits, such as rhubarb, or peaches.

1 Heat the oven to 200°C/400°F/Gas mark 6.

2 Make the stewed apples: Peel the apples and cut them into quarters. Discard the cores. Chop the quarters into pieces.

3 Melt the butter in a saucepan set over gentle heat and add the sugar and apple pieces. Stir well. Cover with a lid and cook for about 10 minutes, stirring from time to time.

4 When the apple is soft, remove from the heat. Taste to see if the apple is sweet enough and add more sugar if not. Grate lemon zest (about half of the lemon) into the apple, and stir well. Taste to see if it is lemony enough.

5 Make the crumble: Place the flour and cinnamon or ginger, if using, into the bowl.

6 Cut the butter into tiny pieces about the size of your little fingernail, add them to the flour and mix around so they are coated in flour. With your fingertips pick up some of the mixture and rub it together between your fingertips. Repeat this process again and again until the mixture looks like coarse breadcrumbs.

7 Stir in the sugar.

8 Place the stewed apple in the ovenproof dish, then spread the crumble topping evenly over the apple.

9 Place the dish on an oven tray in the centre of the oven and bake for about 25–30 minutes, or until it is golden and crisp.

10 Serve warm with milk, cream or ice cream.

Filo Apple Pie

Serves 4

Ingredients:

2 tablespoons raisins (optional)

1 recipe stewed apple (see page 88)

15–30 g (½–1 oz) tablespoons butter

4–5 sheets filo pastry

cream, plain yogurt or vanilla ice cream
   for serving

Equipment:

1 tablespoon

1 ovenproof dish, 1 litre (1¾ pints) capacity

1 small saucepan or bowl

1 pastry brush

1 oven tray

Made with filo pastry, this version of apple pie is very light and it looks most impressive.

1 Heat the oven to 180°C/350°F/Gas mark 4.

2 Stir the raisins, if using, into the cooked apple, then place the apple in an ovenproof dish and spread out.

3 Melt the butter gently, either in a small saucepan or in a small bowl in the microwave.

4 Remove the filo sheets from their packet and place them flat in a pile on top of each other. (Immediately wrap up the rest of the filo pastry so it won't dry out.) Brush the top sheet of pastry on one side with melted butter. Scrunch up the pastry as if you were loosely screwing up paper and place it buttery side up on top of the apple. Repeat this process 3–4 times with the remaining pile of pastry. The top of the apple should be completely covered with scrunched-up pastry.

5 Put the dish on an oven tray in the oven and bake for about 15 minutes until the pastry is golden and crisp.

6 Serve warm, with cream, vanilla ice cream or yogurt, if you like.

Chocolate Mousse

Serves 4-5

Ingredients:

115 g (4 oz) dark (bittersweet) chocolate

4 eggs

Equipment:

3 medium bowls

eggbeater

1 spatula

1 metal spoon

1 medium saucepan

plastic food wrap (cling film)

1 serving bowl or 4–5 individual dishes

If Alexandra has a signature dish, chocolate mousse is surely it. For the absolute best chocolate mousse, use good quality dark (not milk) chocolate, with a high percentage of cocoa.

1 Chop or break the chocolate into small even-sized pieces, place in one of the bowls and melt.*

2 Separate the eggs.* Place the egg whites into one clean bowl and the egg yolks into another clean bowl.

3 Beat the egg whites until they are stiff.*

4 Scrape the egg yolks, using a spatula, into the melted chocolate, then stir until well combined.

5 Spoon the stiff egg whites onto the chocolate mixture, then gently fold* into the mixture with a large metal spoon. When there are no lumps of egg white visible, spoon or pour the mixture into the serving dish or dishes. Cover with plastic food wrap and place in the refrigerator for at least 4 hours to set.

*See How To on pages 16-18.

Chocolate Cake

Serves 8

Ingredients:

oil, for greasing the tin

125 g (4½ oz) self-raising (self-rising) flour

pinch of salt

45 g (1½ oz) unsweetened cocoa powder

165 g (5½ oz) butter

165 g (5½ oz) caster (superfine) sugar

3 eggs

3–4 drops vanilla extract

3 tablespoons warm water

Equipment:

1 round cake tin (pan), 20 cm (8 in) diameter

baking paper

kitchen scales and measures

1 sifter

1 large bowl

1 medium saucepan

1 wooden spoon

1 tablespoon

1 spatula

1 oven tray

1 wire rack

1 kitchen knife

Chocolate cake is our favourite. This version is both scrumptious and easy to make. It is great plain or iced – to make it super chocolatey, ice it with the Chocolate Sauce or Simple Chocolate Icing on page 96.

1 Heat the oven to 180°C/350°F/Gas mark 4.

2 To prepare the cake tin, place the tin on top of some baking paper, draw around the tin, then cut out the circle of paper. Brush the insides of the tin with oil, or wipe it with an oily paper towel, then place the circle of paper in the base of the tin.

3 Sift the flour, salt and cocoa powder into the bowl.

4 Melt the butter in the saucepan over a medium heat. Remove from the heat and add the sugar, eggs and vanilla extract, then stir with a wooden spoon until combined.

5 Pour the butter mixture into the flour mixture and stir until completely combined.

6 Add the warm water and stir again.

7 Pour the mixture into the prepared cake tin, using the spatula to scrape the sides of the bowl.

8 Place the cake tin on the oven tray on a rack in the centre of the oven and bake for about 25 minutes, then test to see if it is cooked. (One test is to insert a fine skewer or sharp knife into the middle of the cake; if it comes out clean then the cake is cooked. Another test is to press lightly with a finger on the top of the cake; if the top springs back the cake is cooked.) When the cake is cooked, remove it from the oven and place the tin on a wire rack to cool. If the cake is not cooked, return to the oven and bake for another 5 minutes before testing again.

9 When the cake is cool, slide the blade of a knife between the cake and the inside edge of the tin and drag it against the tin to loosen, taking care not to cut the cake.

10 Tip the cake tin upside down onto the wire rack, lift the tin off and leave the cake to go cold.

11 If you wish to ice the cake, place a plate upside down over the cold cake and invert, so the cake is on the plate, then ice with Chocolate Sauce or Simple Chocolate Icing on page 96.

Chocolate Sauce

Ingredients:

100 g (3½ oz) dark (bittersweet)
   chocolate

100 ml (3½ fl oz) double (heavy
   whipping) cream

Equipment:

1 small saucepan

1 tablespoon

This is real chocolate sauce and it is divine on ice cream and with fresh fruit or used as a special icing on our Chocolate Cake on page 94 or the Cupcakes on page 102.

1   Chop or break the chocolate into small even-sized pieces.

2   Place the cream in the saucepan and heat it over a low heat until just beginning to boil. Watch it carefully to make sure it does not boil over.

3   As soon as the cream is just boiling, remove from the heat and add to the chocolate. Stir the chocolate into the cream until it is melted.

4   Serve the sauce hot. If the sauce goes cold you can put it in a glass or china dish and gently reheat it in the microwave.

Simple Chocolate Icing

Ingredients:

8 oz (225 g) icing (confectioners')
   sugar

1 tablespoon unsweetened cocoa
   powder

15 g (½ oz) very soft butter

3 tablespoons warm water

Equipment:

1 sieve

1 tablespoon

kitchen scales and measures

1 medium bowl

1 knife

This is another delicious option to top the Chocolate Cake or the Cupcakes.

1   Sift the icing sugar and cocoa powder into the bowl.

2   Add the butter.

3   Add half of the warm water and stir until well combined. Gradually add more water until the icing is runny enough to spread.

4   Spread the icing on the top of the cake with a knife and leave to set.

Upside-down Caramel Banana Cake

Ingredients:

Base:

100 g (3½ oz) butter
100 g (3½ oz) brown sugar
1 teaspoon vanilla essence
1 firm banana (optional)

Cake:

100 g (3 ½ oz) butter
3 eggs
150 ml (5 fl oz) natural yoghurt
100 g (3½ oz) brown sugar
3 ripe bananas
250 g (8¾ oz) plain (all-purpose) flour
3 teaspoons baking powder
1 teaspoon ground cinnamon
oil for brushing tin

Equipment:

22 cm (8½ in) diameter round ring
   cake tin *
1 pastry brush
baking paper
kitchen scales and measures
1 small saucepan
1 large bowl
2 medium-sized bowls
1 egg-beater or whisk
1 sieve
1 wooden spoon
1 spatula
1 fork
1 knife
1 oven tray

*if you use a 20cm (8 in) cake tin, cook
the cake a little longer.

This banana cake is special. It looks great, tastes delicious, and is really easy to make. The caramel base is an instant icing or sauce. Serve it warm as a dessert or cold as a cake.

1 Heat the oven to 180°C /350°F/Gas mark 4.

2 To prepare the cake tin, place the tin onto baking paper, draw around the outside of the tin, including the hole in the middle, then cut out the paper to the ring shape. Brush the insides of the tin with oil, or wipe it with an oily paper towel, then place the paper ring in the bottom of the tin (see step-by-step pictures on page 95).

3 To make the base, melt the butter and sugar in a small saucepan. Stir in vanilla essence and mix until well combined. Pour this mixture into the cake tin and spread it evenly over the bottom.

4 (optional) Slice the banana into circles about ½ cm (¼ in) thick. Arrange the slices on top of the buttery mixture. Set aside.

5 Melt the butter for the cake mixture in the small saucepan.

6 Crack the eggs into a large bowl and whisk until they are slightly frothy.

7 Stir in the yoghurt, melted butter and sugar.

8 Slice the bananas into a bowl, and mash them against the sides of the bowl with the back of a fork until they are a pulp. Stir into the egg mixture.

9 Sift the flour, baking powder and cinnamon into the egg mixture, and stir with a wooden spoon until just combined.

10 Pour into the cake tin on top of the base, using the spatula to scrape out the sides of the bowl.

11 Place the cake tin on the oven tray on a rack in the centre of the oven and bake for about 50 minutes then test to see if it is cooked. (One test is to insert a fine skewer into the middle

of the cake; if it comes out clean then the cake is cooked.) When the cake is cooked, remove it from the oven and rest for 5 minutes. If the cake is not cooked, return it to the oven and bake it for another 5 minutes before testing it again.

12 To serve, slide the blade of a knife between the cake and the inside edge of the cake tin and scrape it against the tin to loosen the cake, taking care not to cut the cake. Place a large plate upside down on top of the cake, then holding onto both the tin and the plate, flip them over so that the plate is underneath the cake. The cake will unmould onto the plate.

Chocolate Truffles

Makes about 35

Ingredients:

250 g (9 oz) dark (bittersweet) chocolate

100 ml (3½ fl oz) single (light) cream

3 drops vanilla extract

15 g (½ oz) unsalted
    butter, softened

unsweetened cocoa powder/icing
    (confectioners') sugar

Equipment:

1 medium bowl

kitchen scales and measures

1 small saucepan

1 tablespoon

2 small bowls

1 wooden spoon

plastic food wrap (cling film)

1 teaspoon

1 sieve

We make these absolutely scrumptious chocolate truffles to give as gifts at Christmas. Dust them in icing sugar if you don't like powdered cocoa.

1 Break or chop the chocolate into small even-sized pieces, then place in the medium bowl and melt.* When the chocolate is melted, set it aside to cool.

2 Place the cream in the saucepan over a low heat until almost boiling — bubbles will just begin to appear around the edge of the cream. Remove from the heat and add the vanilla extract.

3 In one of the small bowls, beat the butter with the wooden spoon until it is very soft.

4 Stir the butter into the cooled chocolate, then stir in the cream mixture. Stir until all the ingredients are combined well. Cover with plastic food wrap and refrigerate for a couple of hours until the mixture is firm enough to roll but not too hard.

5 After making sure your hands are clean, scoop out a teaspoon of the firm chocolate mixture, and roll it between the palms of both hands into a ball. Repeat until you have about 10 balls (it is easier to do in batches).

6 Sift some cocoa powder or icing sugar into the second small bowl. One at a time, roll each ball of chocolate mixture in the cocoa powder or icing sugar to coat the outside evenly.

7 Repeat the rolling and coating process until all of the mixture is used.

8 Carefully place the truffles in a container and cover. Store in the refrigerator until you are ready to serve them.

***See How To on page 18.**

Cupcakes

Makes 12

Ingredients:

125 g (4½ oz) butter

125 g (4½ oz) caster (superfine) sugar

½ teaspoon vanilla essence

125 g (4½ oz) self-raising (self-rising) flour

2 large eggs

3 tablespoons milk

Equipment:

12 paper muffin cases

1 muffin tray

kitchen scales and measures

2 medium bowls

1 sieve

1 wooden spoon or electric mixer

1 cup

1 metal tablespoon

2 teaspoons

1 wire rack

These individual cakes were the first thing that I learned to bake when I was a child. They are delightfully light and moist and I prefer them just as they are. However, you can ice them – perhaps use the Chocolate Sauce or Chocolate Icing recipes.

1 Heat the oven to 180°C/350°F/Gas mark 4.

2 Place the paper cases in the muffin tray hollows.

3 Place the butter in a bowl and soften it if it is hard.* Add the sugar and vanilla extract and beat together with a wooden spoon or electric mixer until smooth and well combined. This is called 'creaming'.

4 Sift the flour into the other bowl.

5 Break one egg into a cup – if any eggshell falls in remove it. Add the egg to the butter mixture and beat well.

6 Stir a spoonful of the sifted flour into the butter mixture. Break the second egg into the cup, add to the butter mixture and beat well.

7 Add the rest of the flour and fold into the mixture with a metal spoon.

8 Add the milk and stir well.

9 Using 2 teaspoons, scoop and scrape the mixture evenly into the paper cases.

10 Bake the cupcakes in the middle of the oven for about 15 minutes until their tops are golden in colour and they spring back when lightly touched.

11 Remove the cupcakes from the oven and cool for a few minutes, then take them out of the muffin tray and spread them on a wire rack to cool. If you want to ice them, wait until they are completely cold.

*See How To on page 18.

Peanut Butter Cookies

Makes about 36

Ingredients:

140 g (5 oz) butter

115 g (4 oz) caster (superfine) sugar

115 g (4 oz) light brown sugar

1 large egg

115 g (4 oz) crunchy peanut butter

½ teaspoon vanilla extract

225 g (8 oz) plain (all-purpose) flour

½ teaspoon salt

1 teaspoon baking powder

Equipment:

3 baking sheets

baking paper

kitchen scales and measures

1 large bowl

1 wooden spoon

electric beaters (optional)

1 cup

1 sifter or sieve

1 medium bowl

1 teaspoon

1 fork

1 wire rack

1 fish slice

Crunchy and peanutty, these biscuits are incredibly delicious, and moreish — obviously you have to like peanut butter to be a fan.

1 Heat the oven to 180°C/350°F/Gas mark 4.

2 Cover the baking sheet with baking paper.

3 Place the butter in the large bowl and soften it if it is hard.＊ Add the sugars to the soft butter and beat them together with the wooden spoon or electric beaters until smooth and well combined. This is called 'creaming'.

4 Break the egg into the cup — if any eggshell falls in remove it. Add the egg to the butter mixture and beat in well, then beat in the peanut butter and the vanilla extract.

5 Sift the flour, salt and baking powder into the other bowl, then add to the butter mixture.

6 Using a wooden spoon, mix everything together until just combined. Do not mix too much or it will become too sticky.

7 Scoop out some mixture with a teaspoon and roll into a ball with your fingers; the mixture is quite soft. Place the balls on the prepared oven trays about 10 cm (4 in) apart. Flatten each ball by pressing with the prongs of a fork. If the fork sticks to the cookies, put a spoonful of flour into a small dish and dip the fork in the flour first.

8 You can bake the first sheet of cookies while you prepare the second tray. Place the tray on a rack in the centre of the oven and bake for 10–12 minutes, until they are an even peanut-brown colour.

9 Remove from the oven. While they are still warm slide a fish slice under each cookies to loosen it, then transfer to a wire rack to cool.

10 When the cookies are completely cold, put them in an airtight container to store.

＊See How To on page 18.

Fruity Oat Slice

Makes 20 pieces

Ingredients:

oil, for greasing the tin
175 g (6 oz) butter
60 ml (2 fl oz) honey
85 g (3 oz) dried apricots
175 g (6 oz) plain (all-purpose) flour
175 g (6 oz) rolled oats
115 g (4 oz) caster (superfine) sugar
100 g (3½ oz) sultanas (golden raisins)
    or raisins
115 g (4 oz) dark (bittersweet)
    chocolate drops

Equipment:

1 low-sided rectangular baking tin (pan),
    measuring 26 x 17 cm (10 x 7 in)
1 pastry brush or paper towel
kitchen scales and measures
1 small saucepan
1 chopping board
1 sharp knife or kitchen scissors (optional)
1 sieve
1 large bowl
1 tablespoon
1 wire rack

This delicious slice is a cross between a muesli bar and a cake — it is perfect for instant energy.

1   Heat the oven to 180°C/350°F/Gas mark 4.
2   Brush the insides of the tin with oil, or wipe it with an oily paper towel.
3   Place the butter and the honey into the small saucepan and gently heat until melted. Set aside.
4   Chop the dried apricots into small pieces about the size of your fingernail. (It may be easier to chop the apricots with kitchen scissors.)
5   Sift the flour into the bowl.
6   Add the oats, sugar, chopped apricots, raisins and chocolate drops to the flour and stir everything together well.
7   Pour the melted butter and honey over the mixture in the bowl and stir until well combined and moist.
8   Spoon the mixture into the prepared tin. Spread it out evenly, then press it down with the back of the spoon.
9   Bake the slice in the middle of the oven for about 20 minutes until it is lightly browned.
10 Remove the slice from the oven and place on a wire rack to cool.
11 When the slice is completely cold, place the clean chopping board on top of the tin, then turn both upside down. Tap gently on the base of the tin and the slice will fall out onto the board. Cut the slice into pieces with a sharp knife.

Index

OCT 2015

US $12.99
UK £9.99